Rosh Hashanah Greeting Cards Coloring Book

By Alex Man

שנה טובה

שנה של בריאות, אושר, הצלחה ואהבה

שנה
טובה

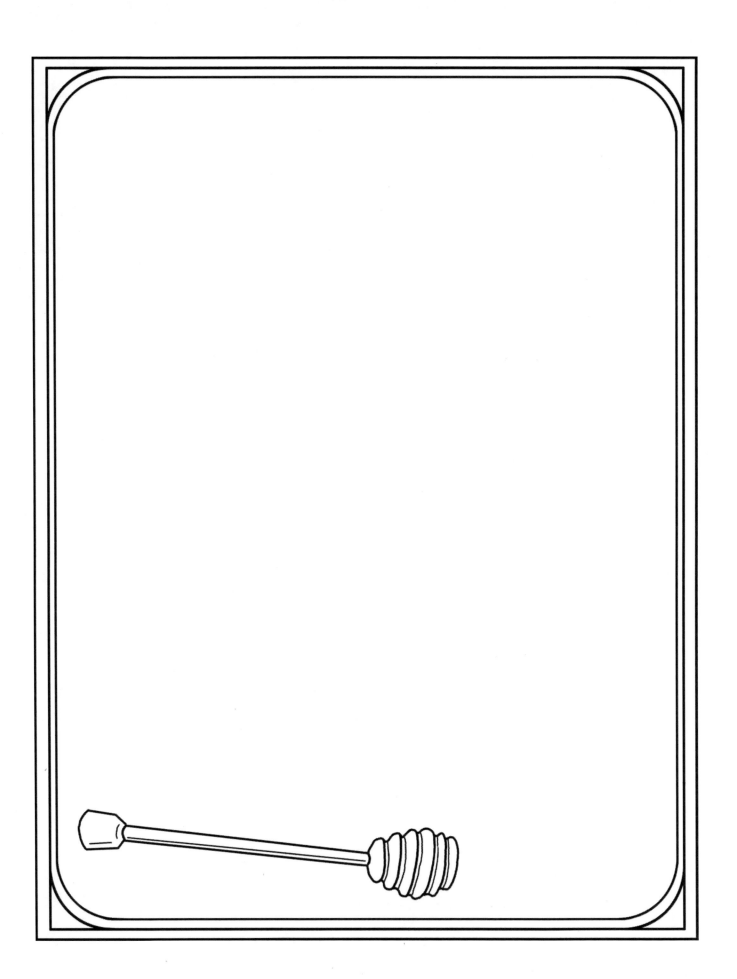

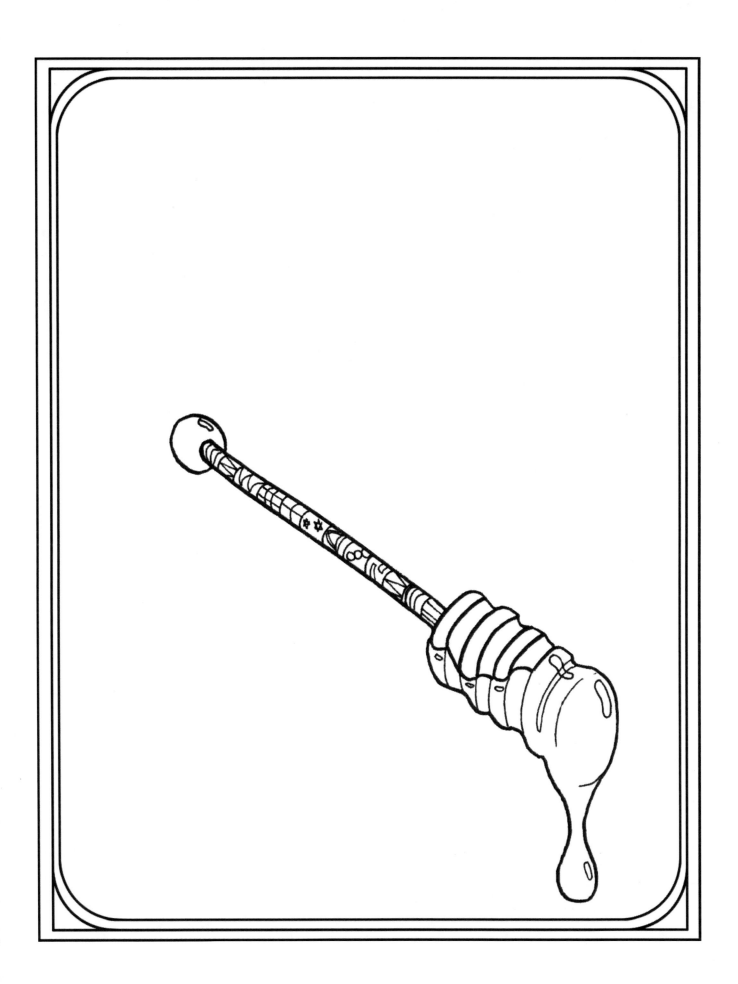

תכלה שנה וקללותיה,
תחל שנה וברכותיה

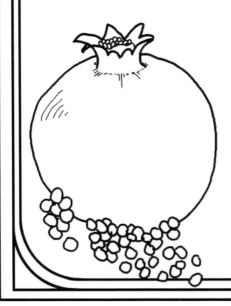

שנה
טובה!

שנה טובה ומתוקה

Instructions for preparing the envelopes

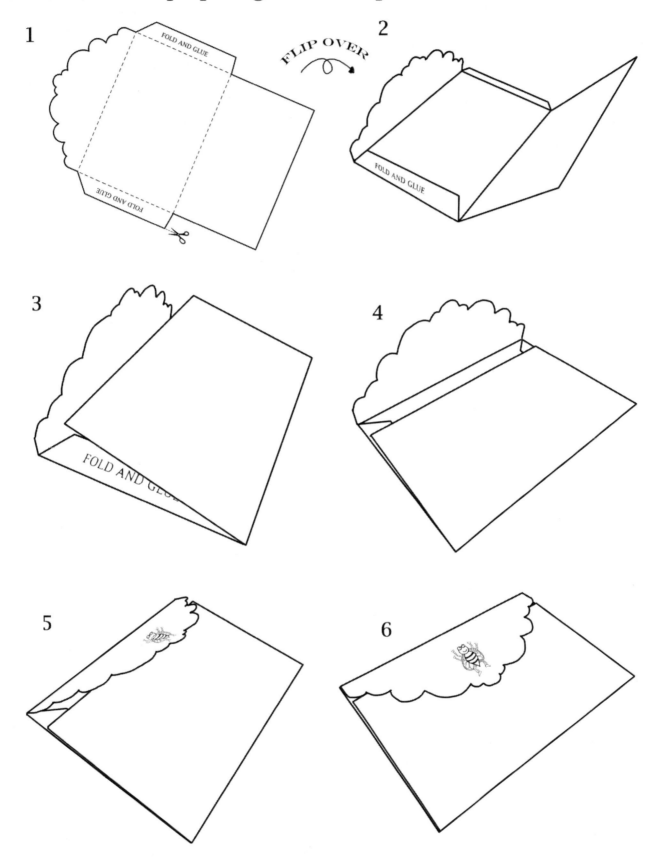

1

FOLD AND GLUE

FOLD AND GLUE

FOLD AND GLUE

FLIP OVER

2

FOLD AND GLUE

3

FOLD AND GLUE

4

5

6

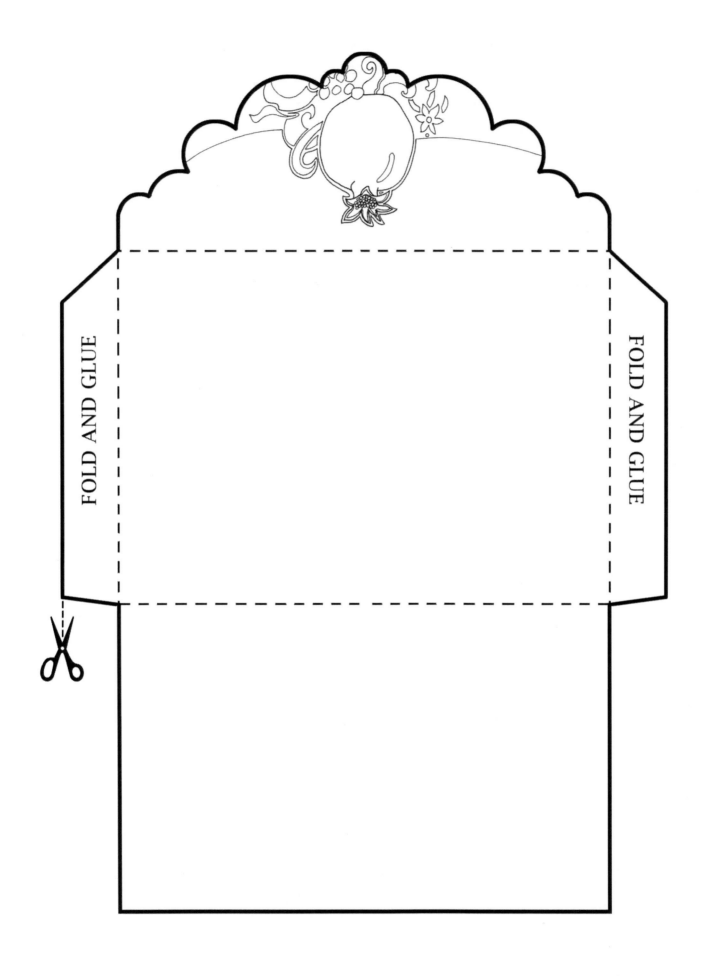

FOLD AND GLUE

FOLD AND GLUE

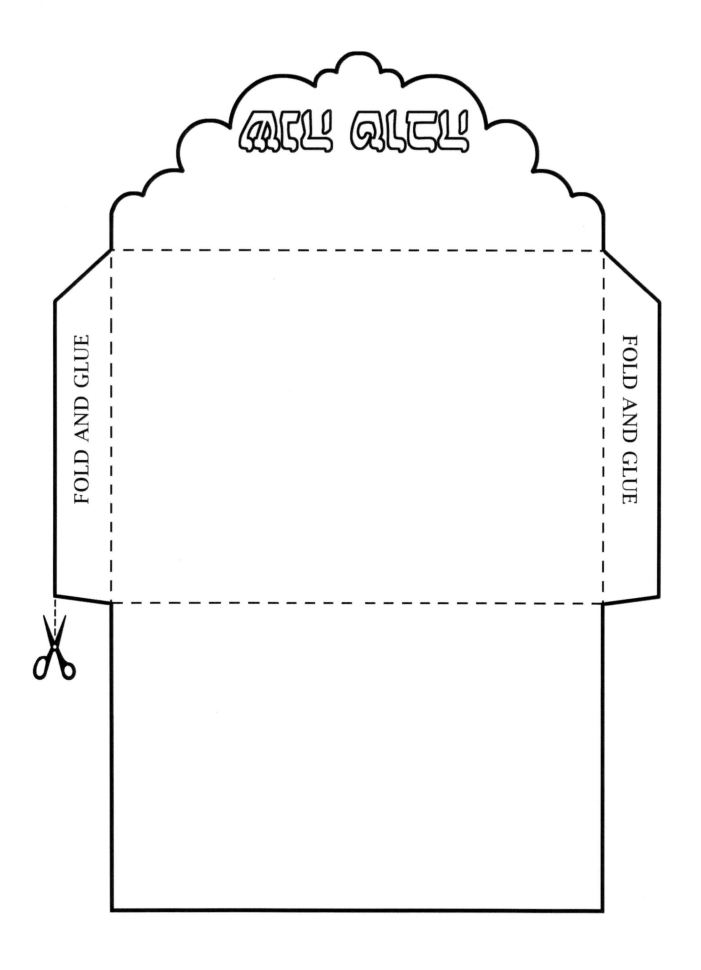

נתַן בָּתַן

FOLD AND GLUE

FOLD AND GLUE

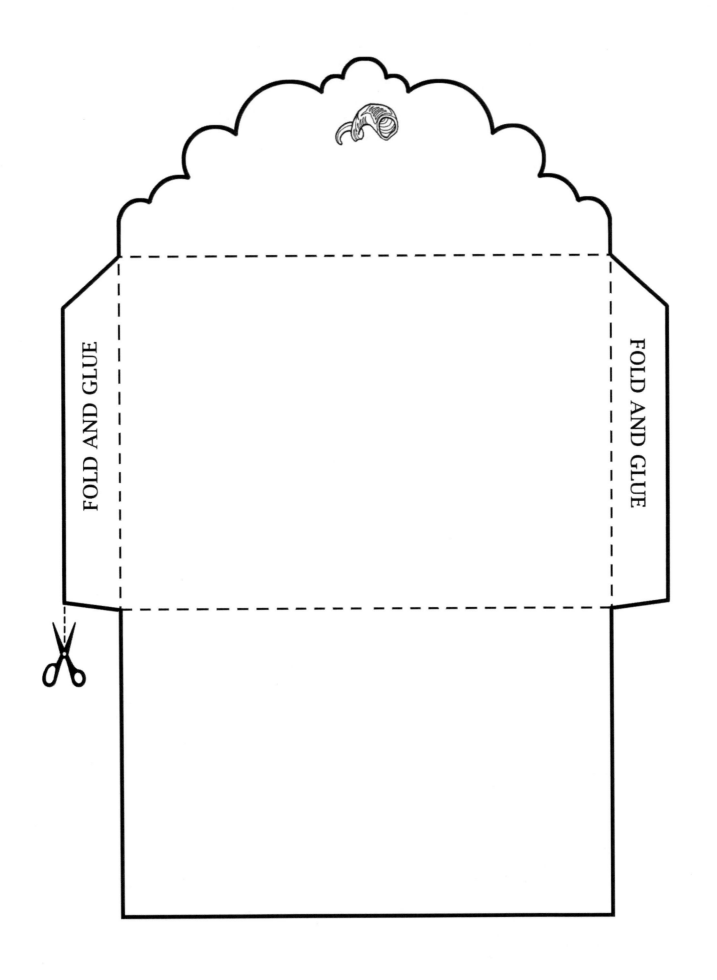

FOLD AND GLUE

FOLD AND GLUE

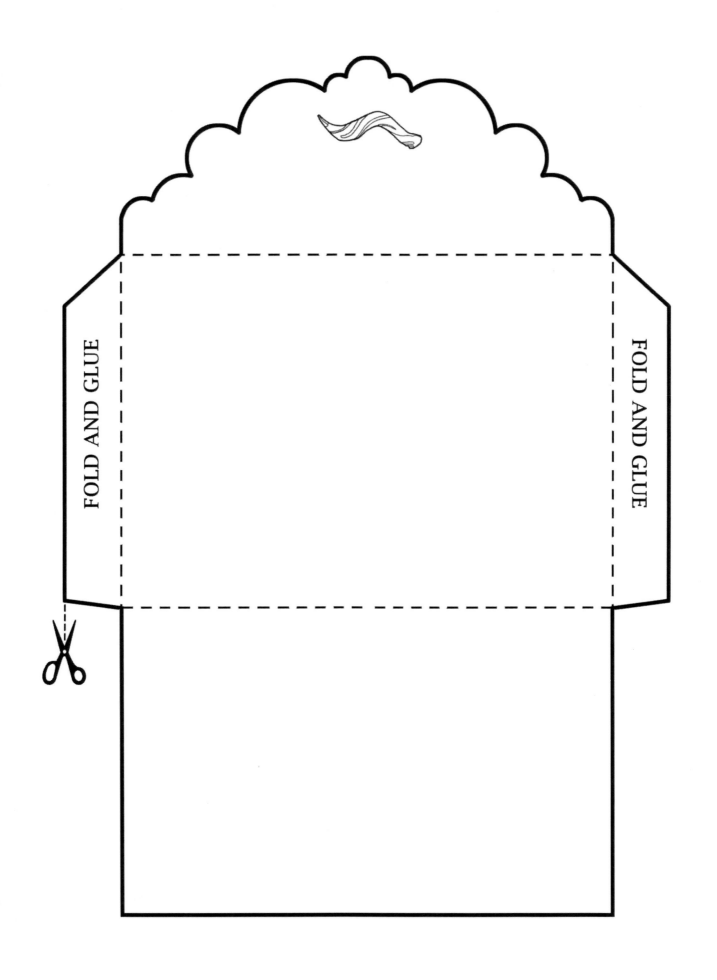

FOLD AND GLUE

FOLD AND GLUE

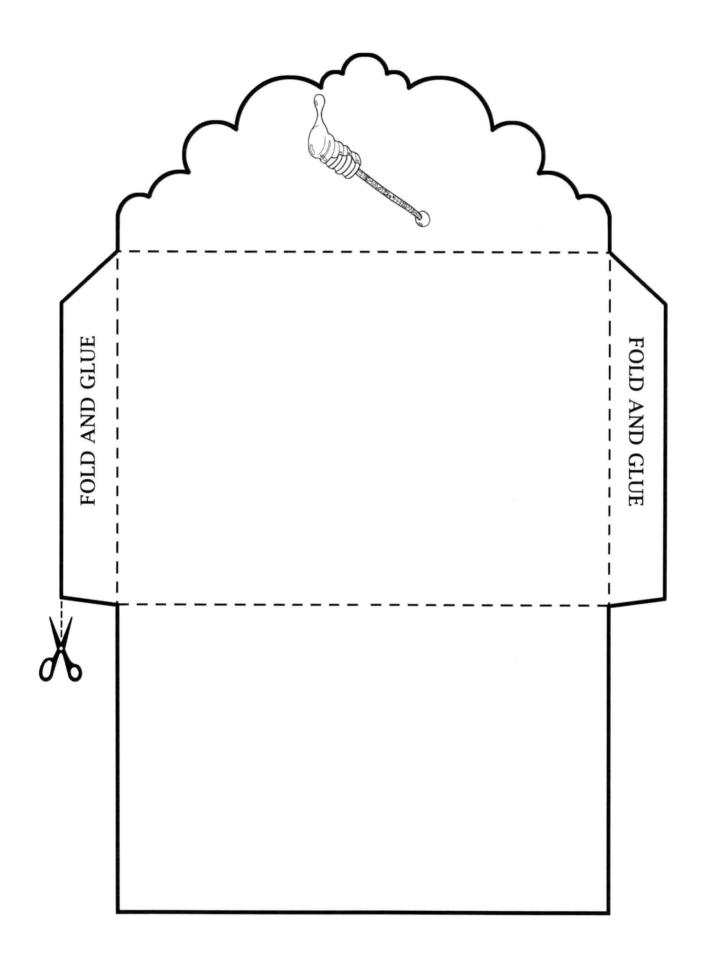

FOLD AND GLUE

FOLD AND GLUE

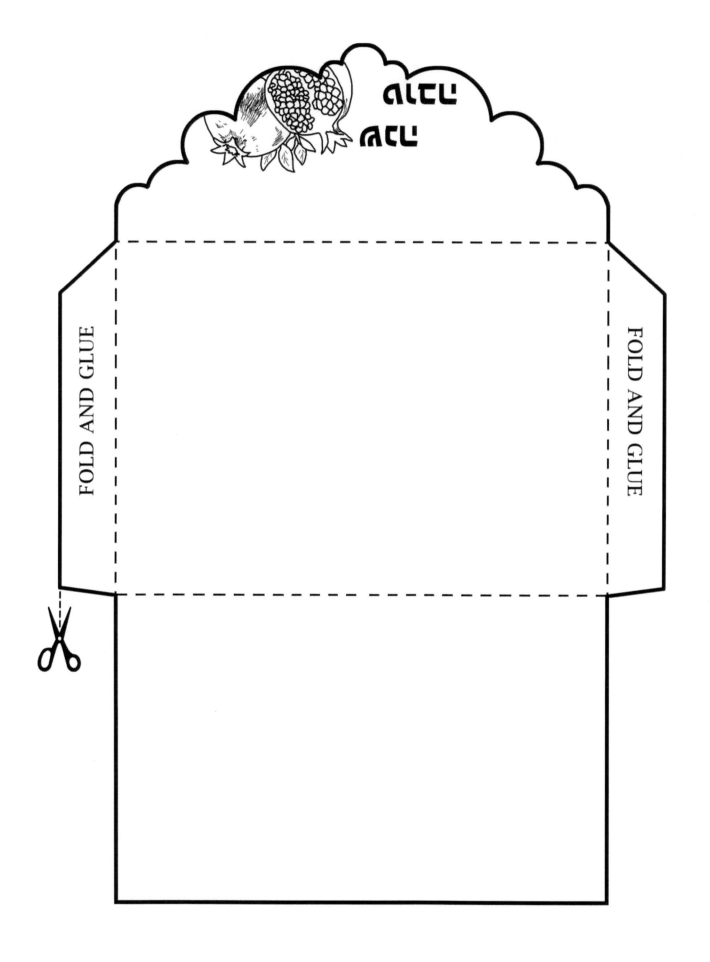

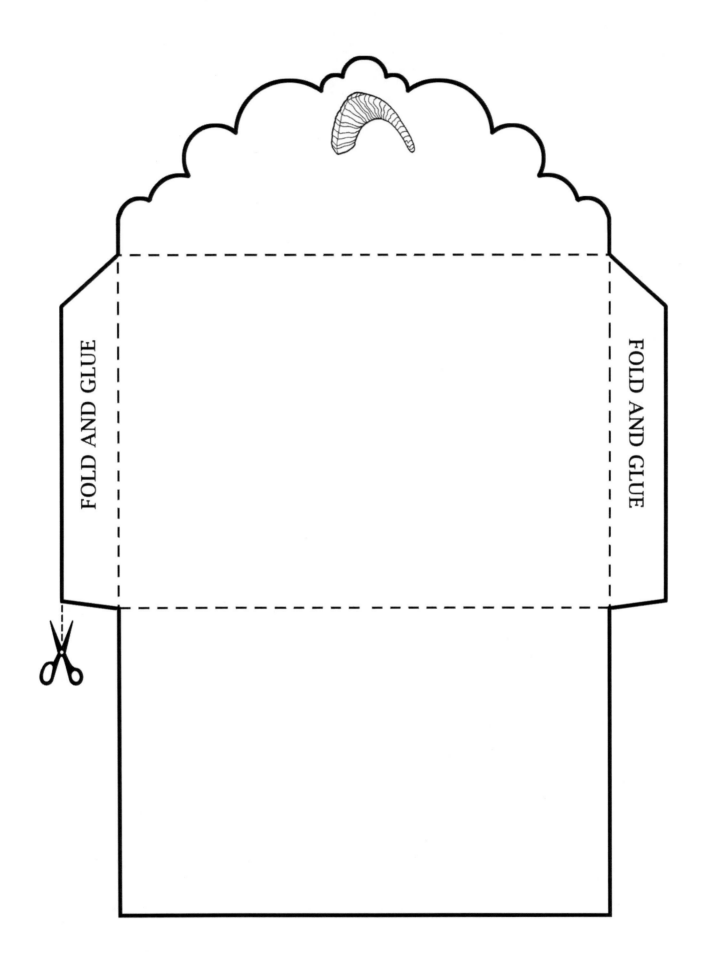

FOLD AND GLUE

FOLD AND GLUE

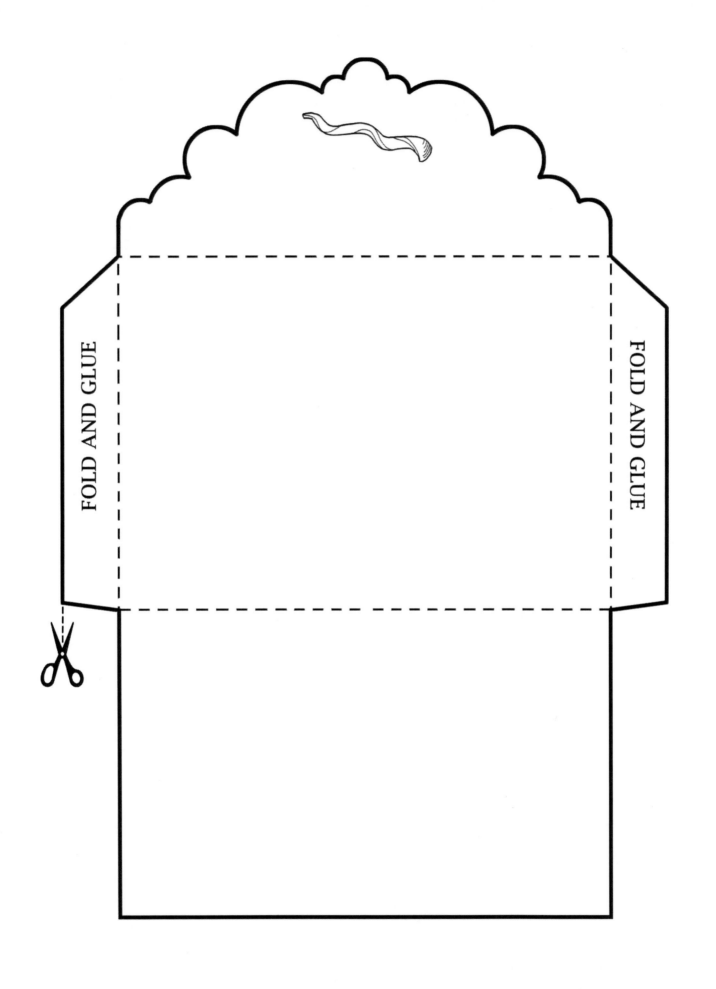

FOLD AND GLUE

FOLD AND GLUE

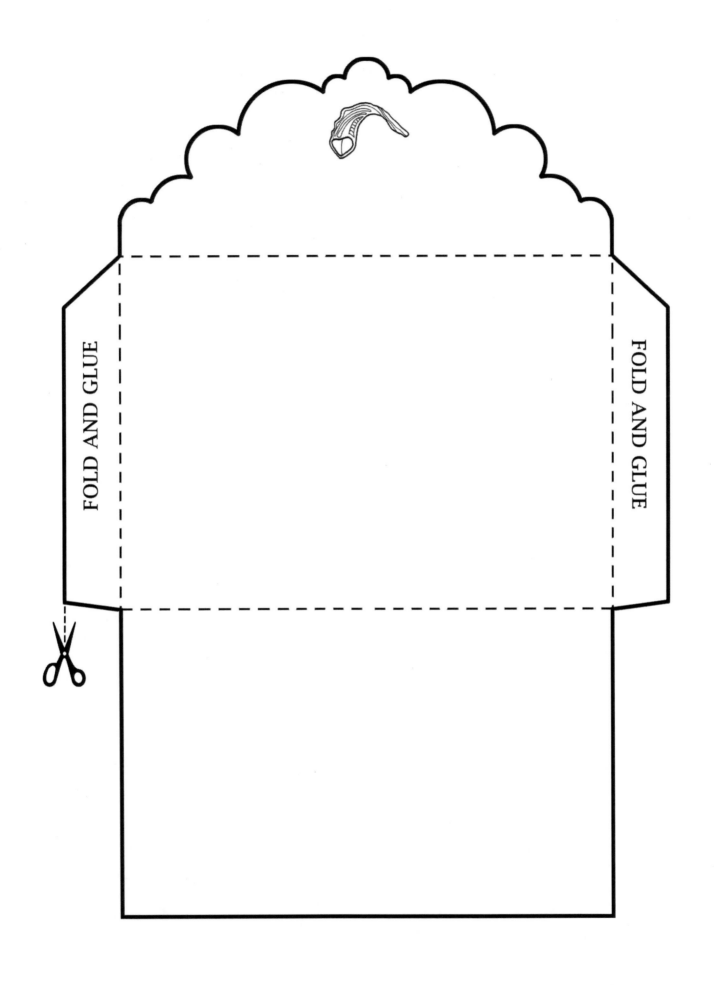

FOLD AND GLUE

FOLD AND GLUE

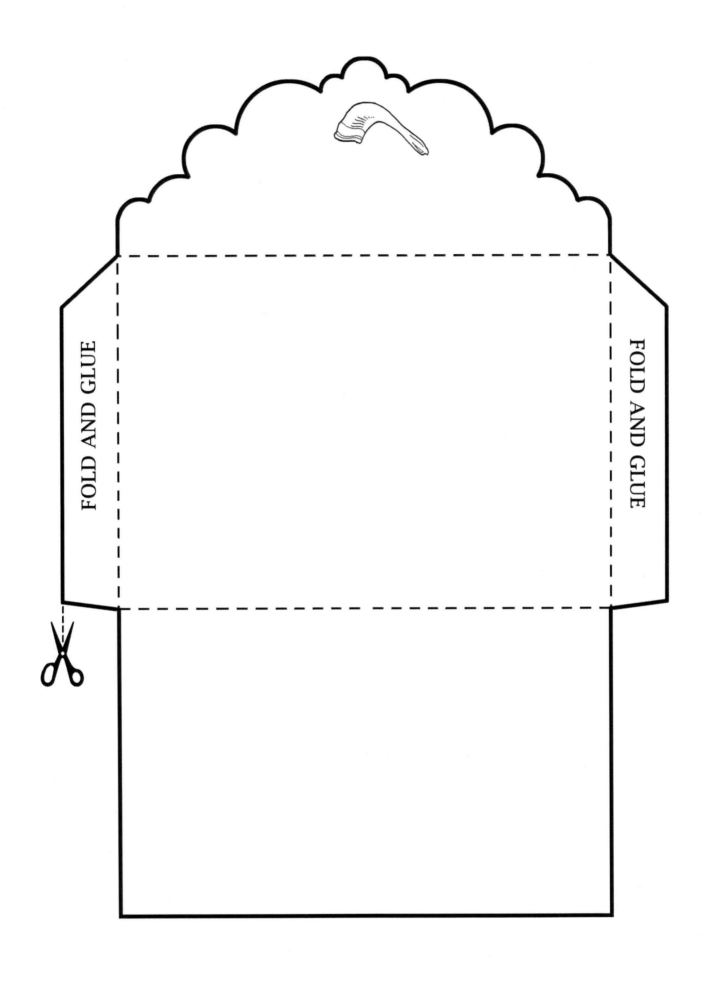

FOLD AND GLUE

FOLD AND GLUE

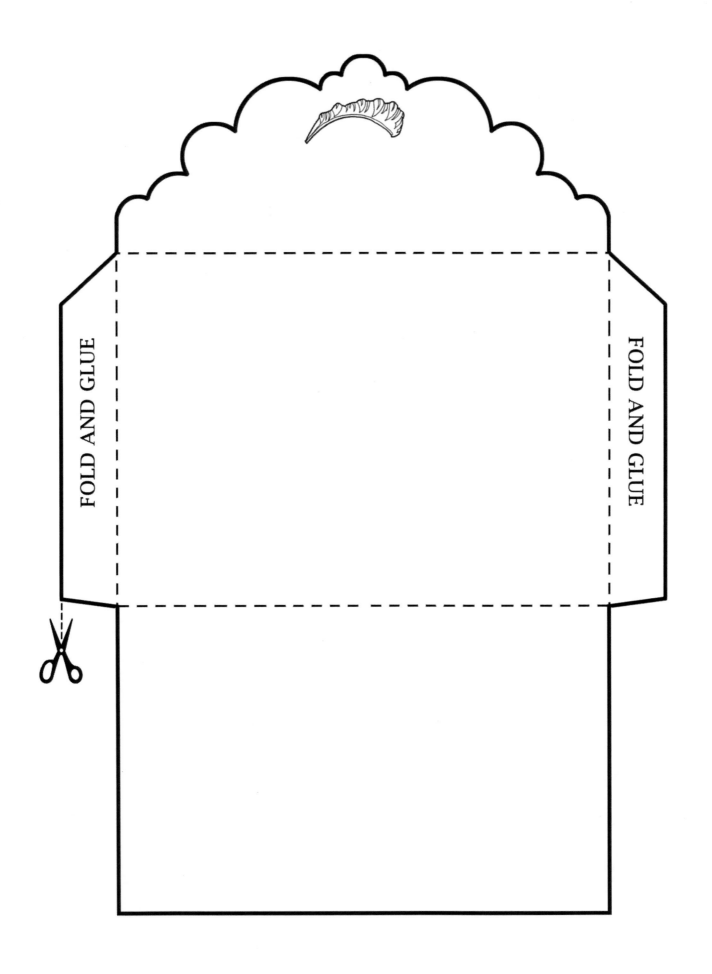

FOLD AND GLUE

FOLD AND GLUE

FOLD AND GLUE

FOLD AND GLUE

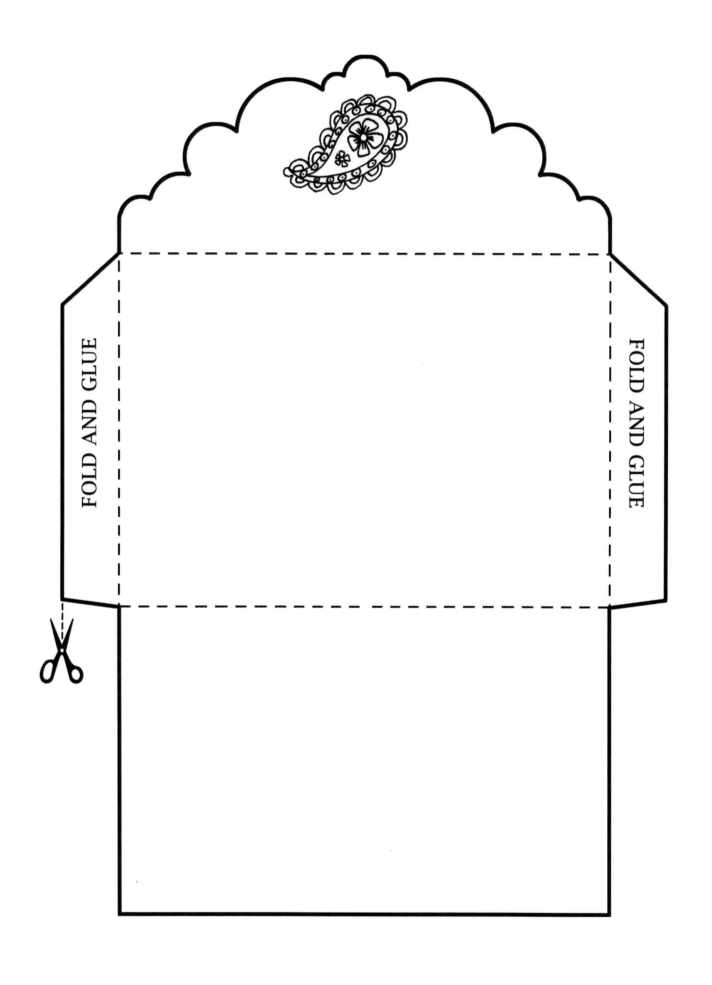

FOLD AND GLUE

FOLD AND GLUE

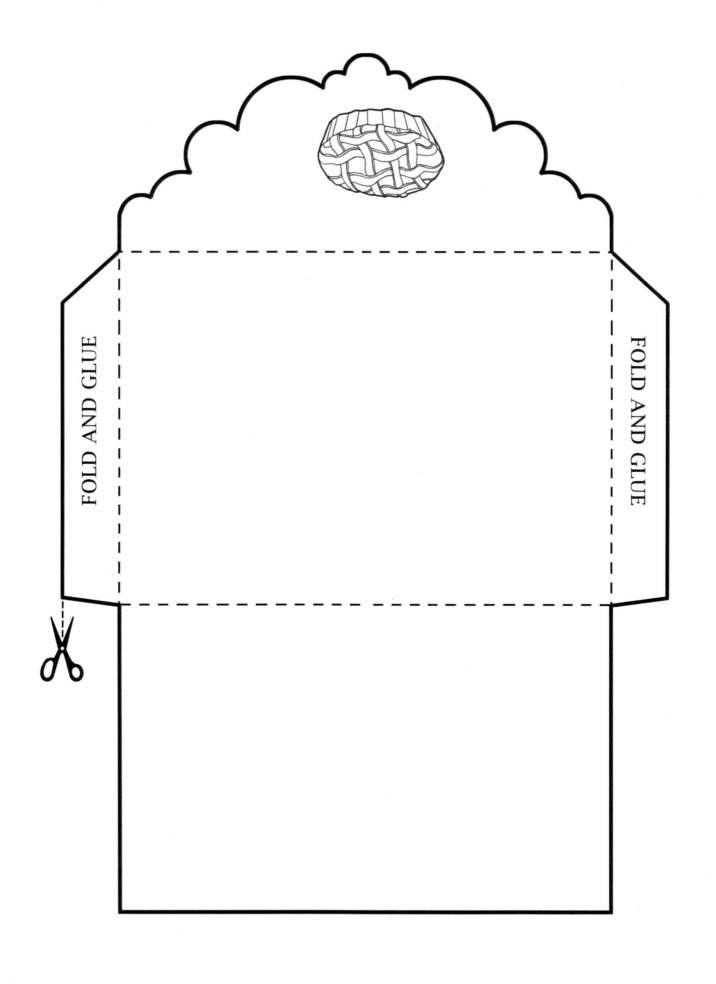

FOLD AND GLUE

FOLD AND GLUE

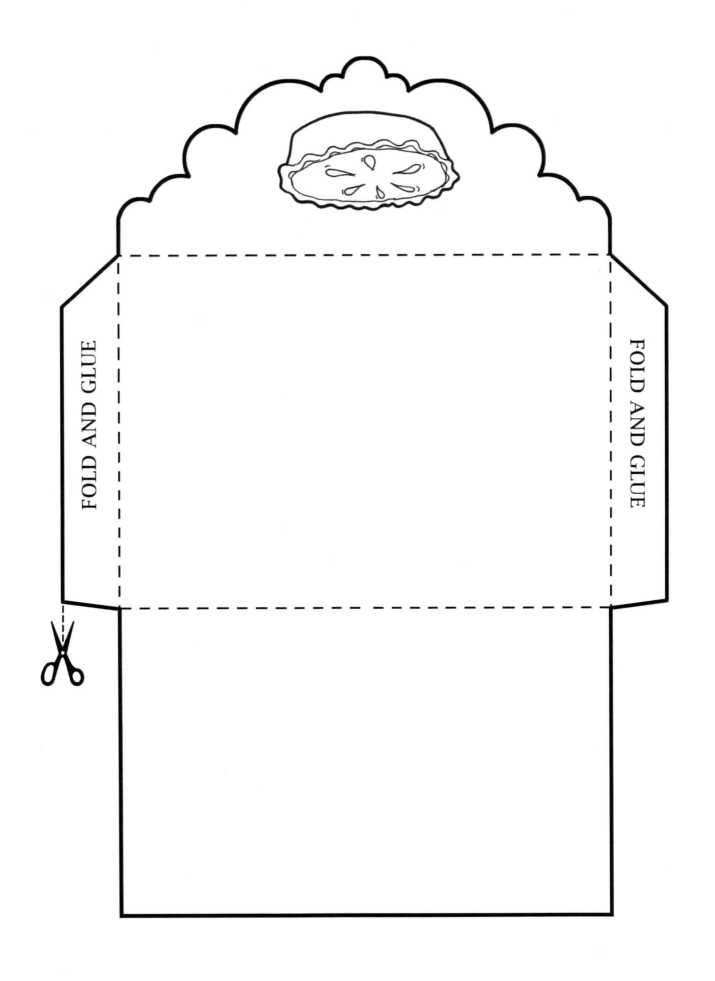

FOLD AND GLUE

FOLD AND GLUE

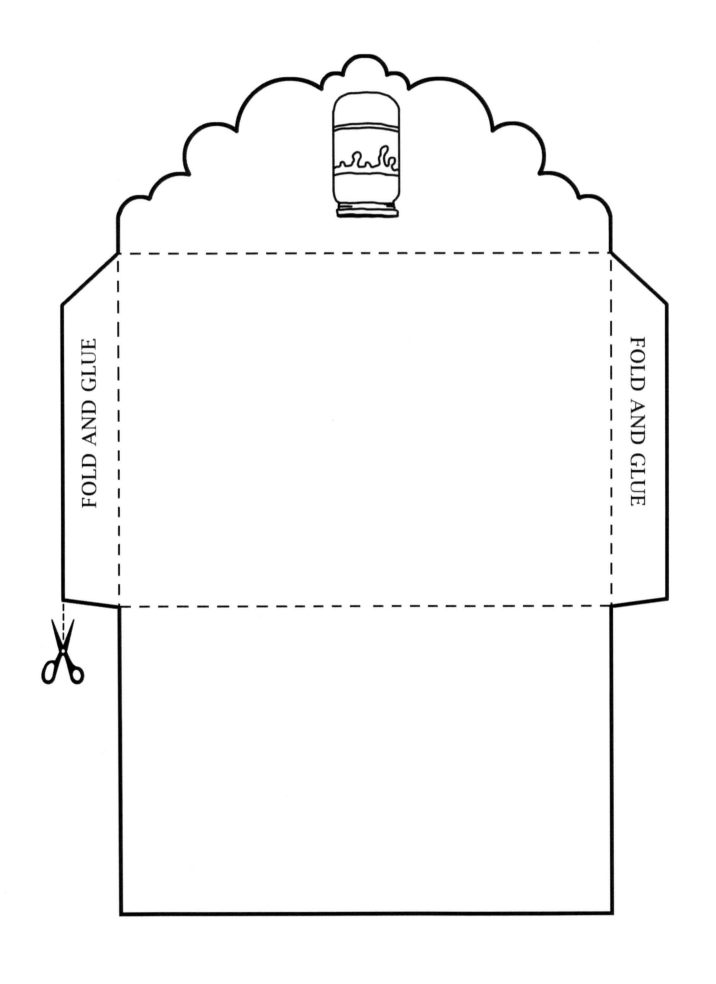

FOLD AND GLUE

FOLD AND GLUE

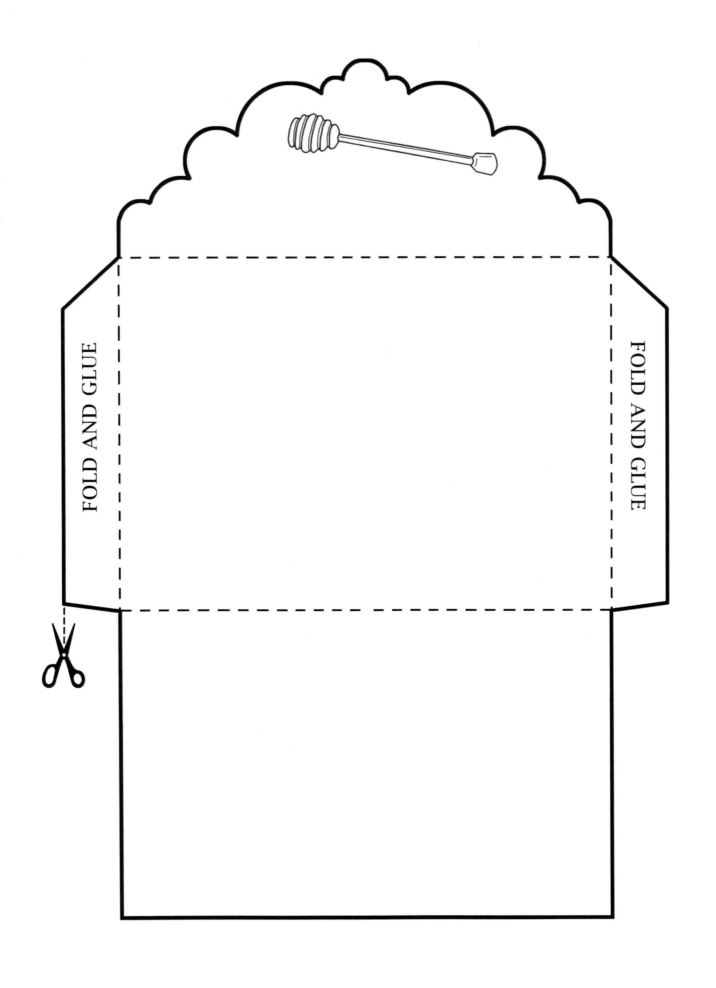

FOLD AND GLUE

FOLD AND GLUE

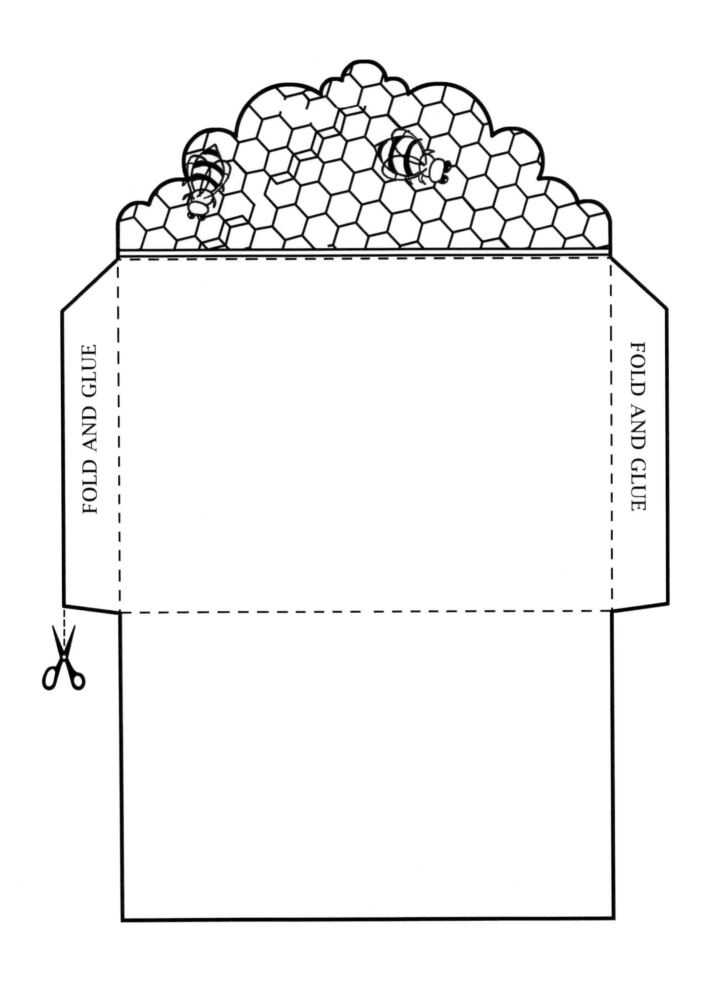

FOLD AND GLUE

FOLD AND GLUE

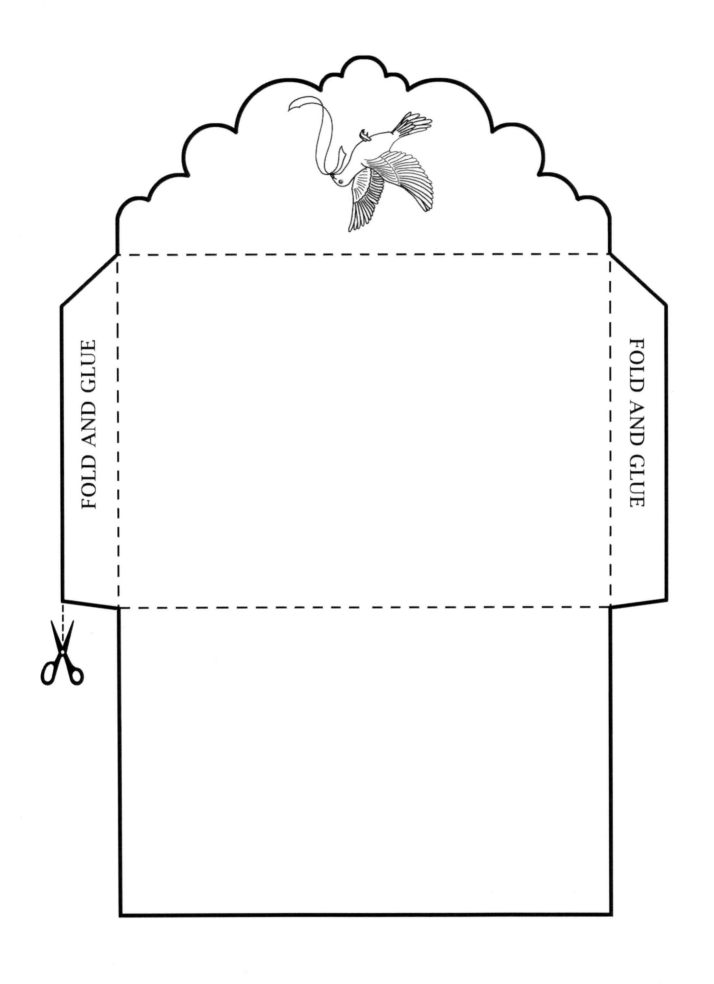

FOLD AND GLUE

FOLD AND GLUE

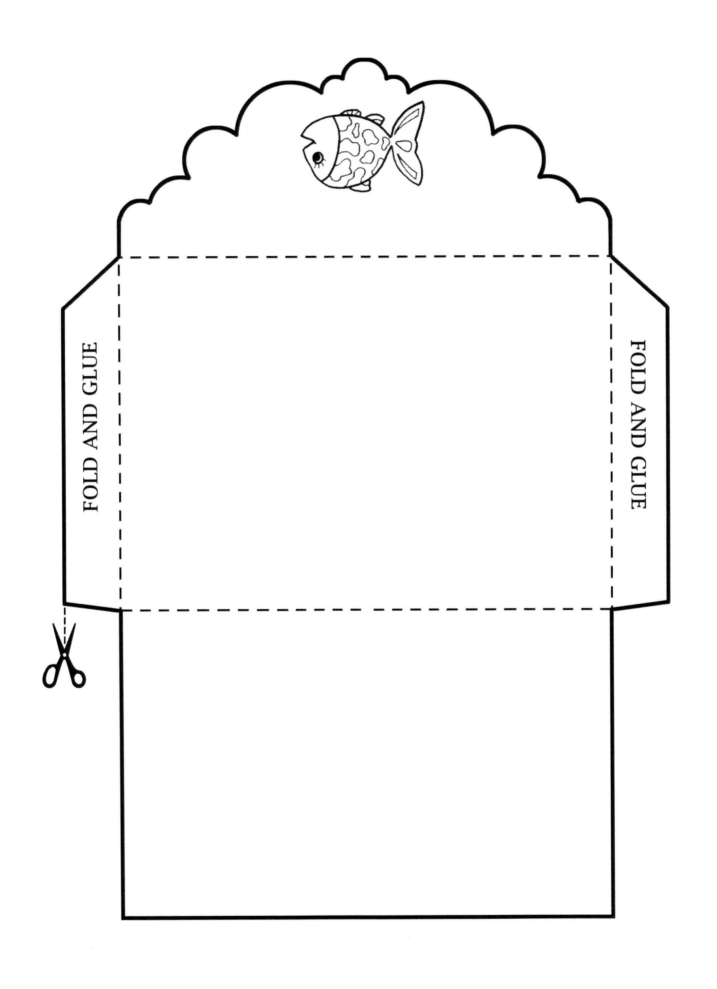

FOLD AND GLUE

FOLD AND GLUE

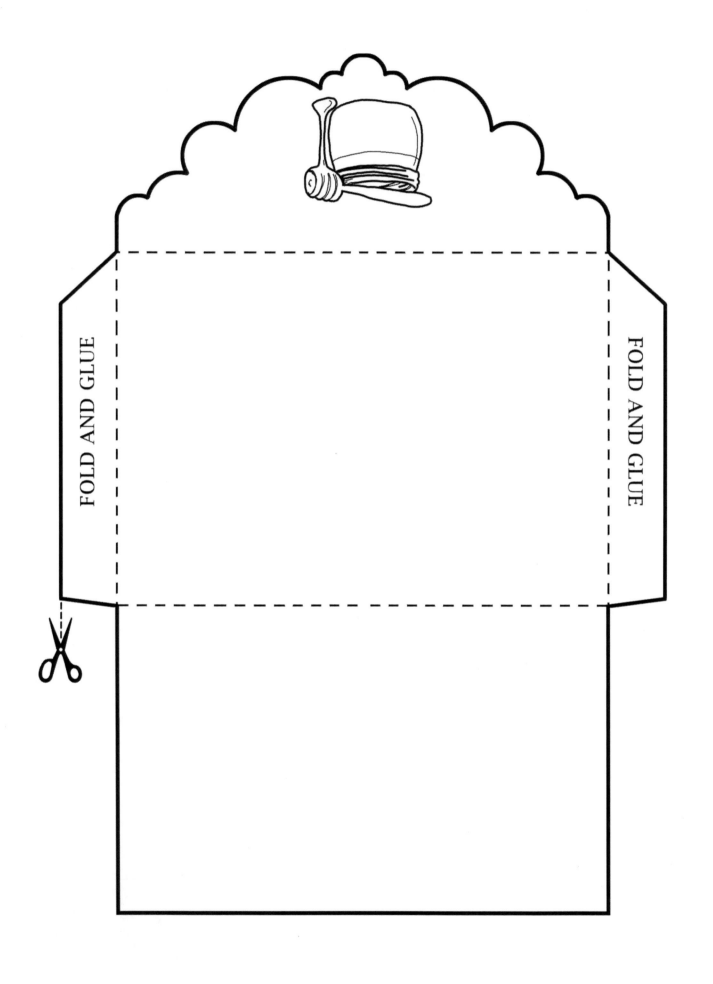

FOLD AND GLUE

FOLD AND GLUE

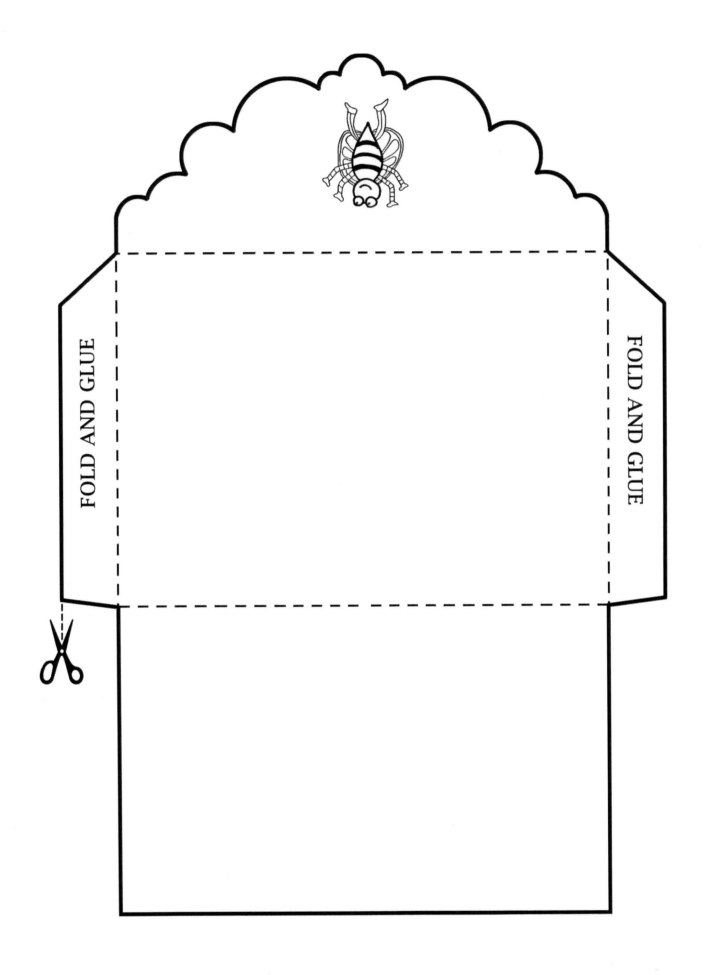

FOLD AND GLUE

FOLD AND GLUE

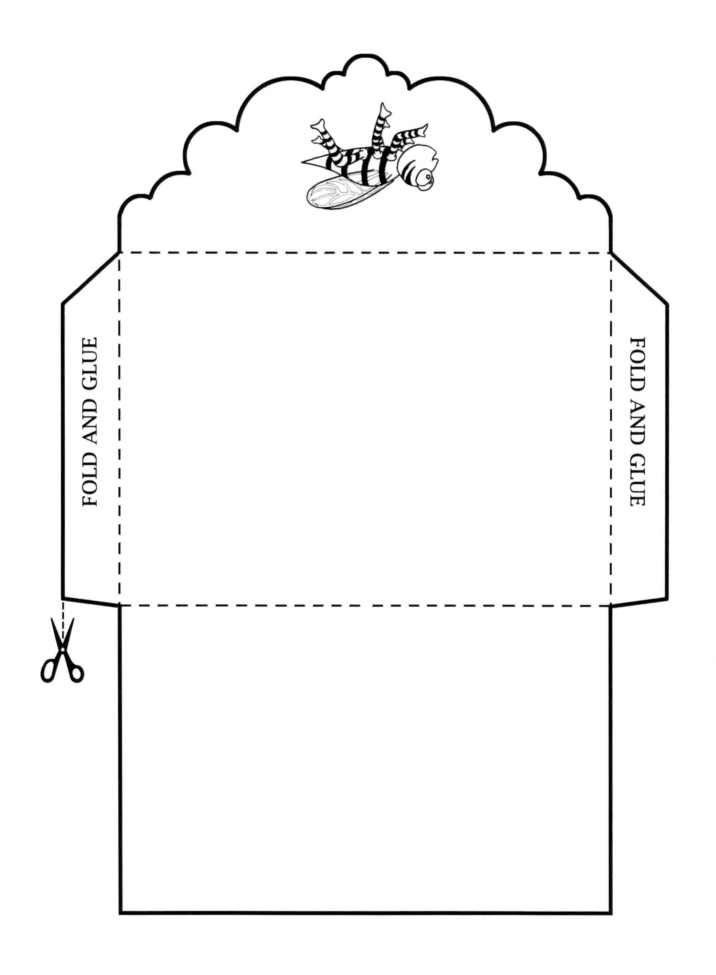

FOLD AND GLUE

FOLD AND GLUE

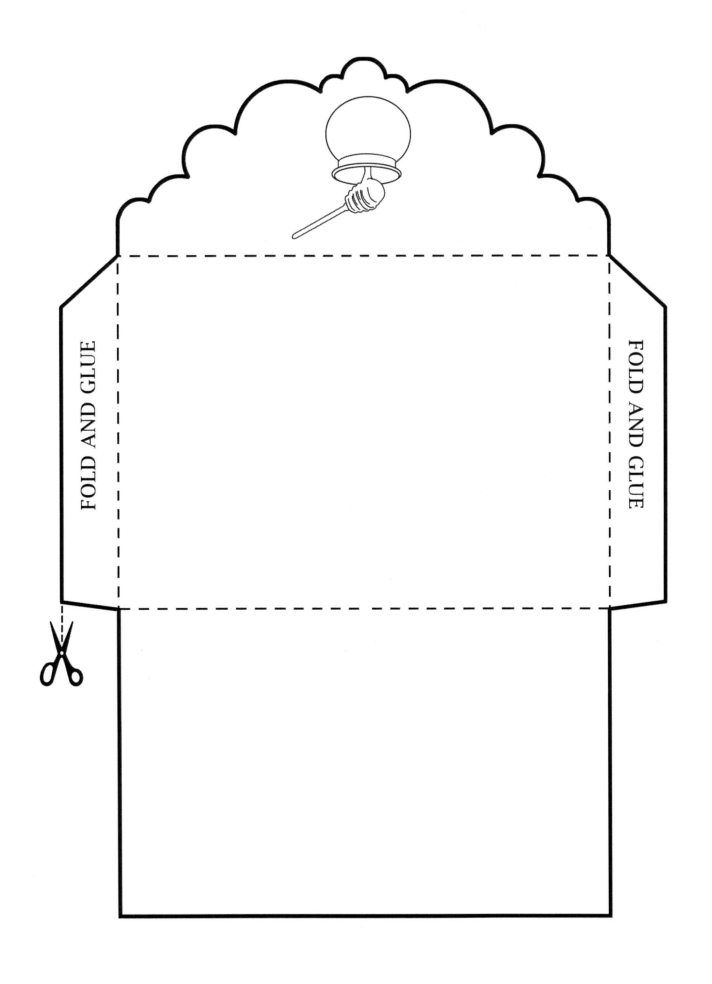

FOLD AND GLUE

FOLD AND GLUE

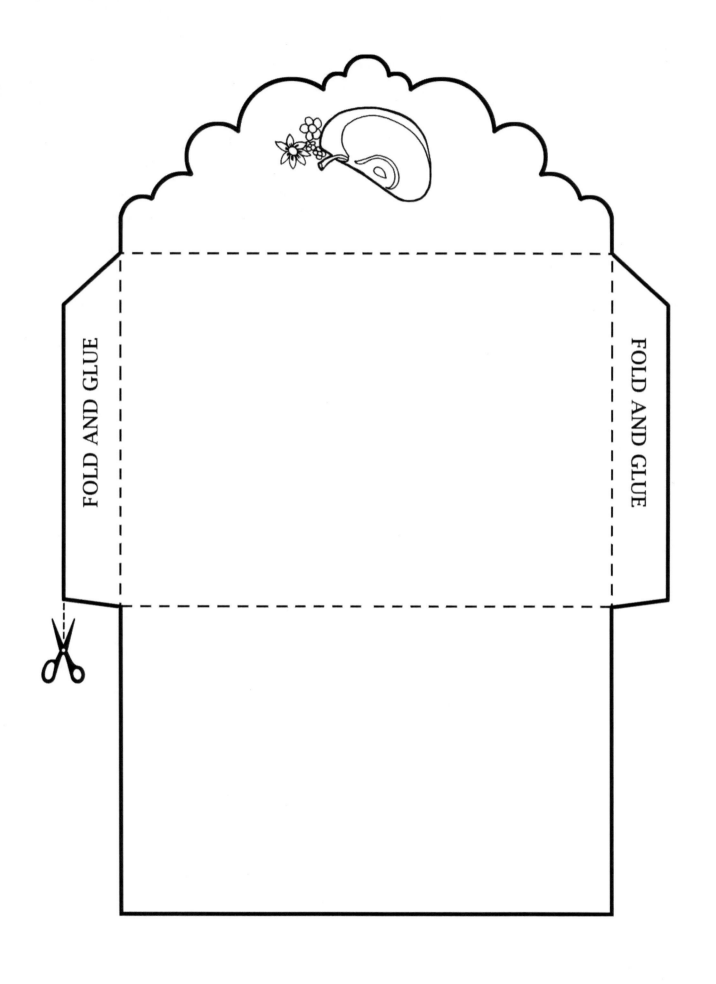

FOLD AND GLUE

FOLD AND GLUE

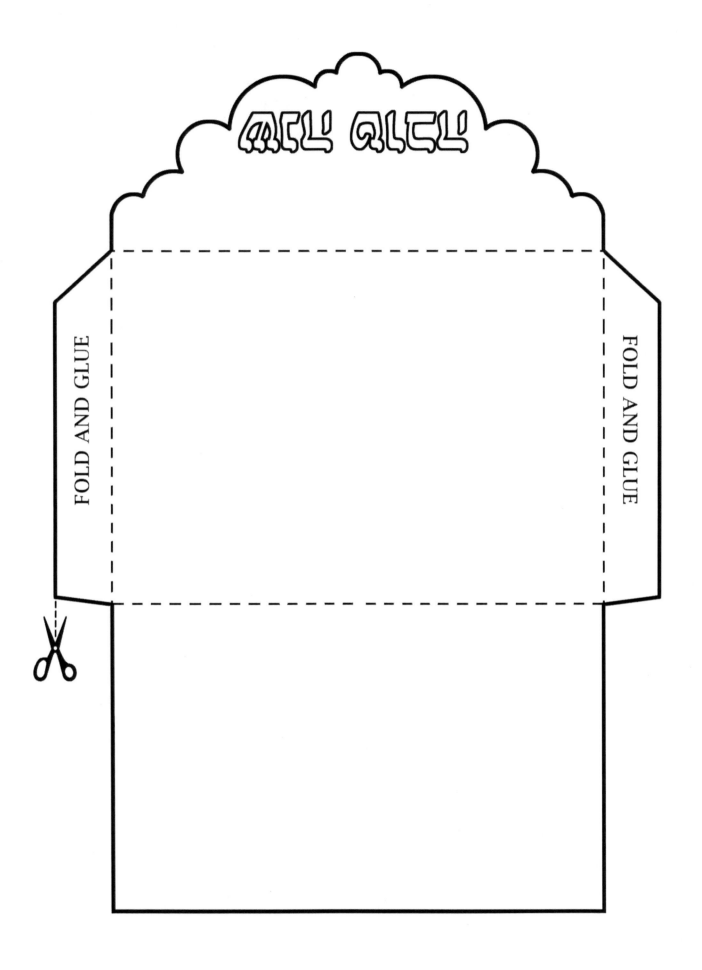

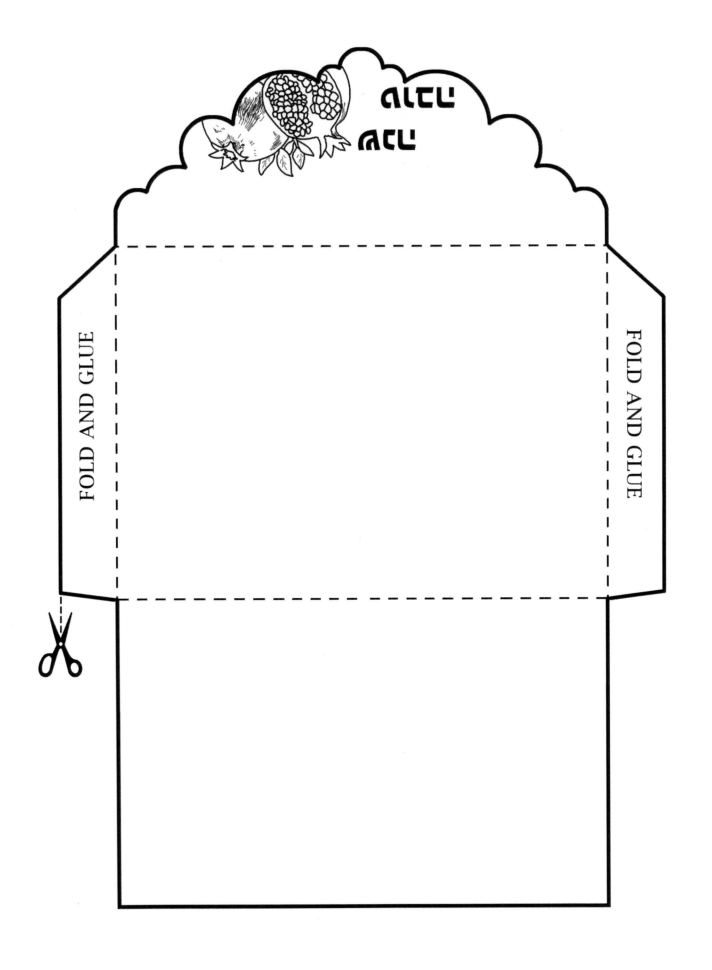

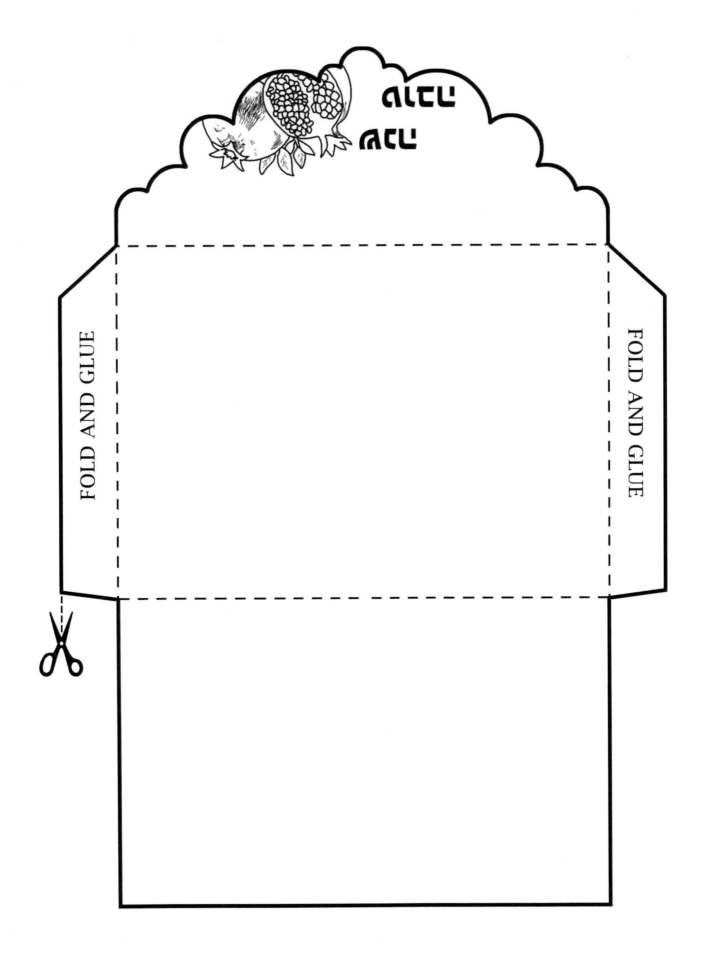

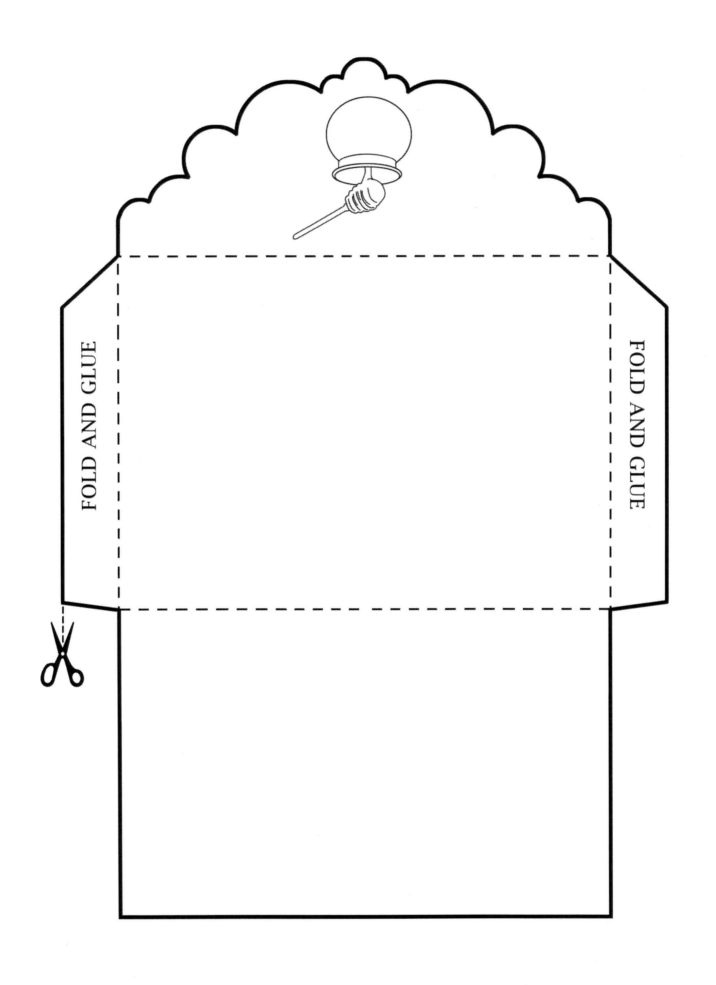

FOLD AND GLUE

FOLD AND GLUE

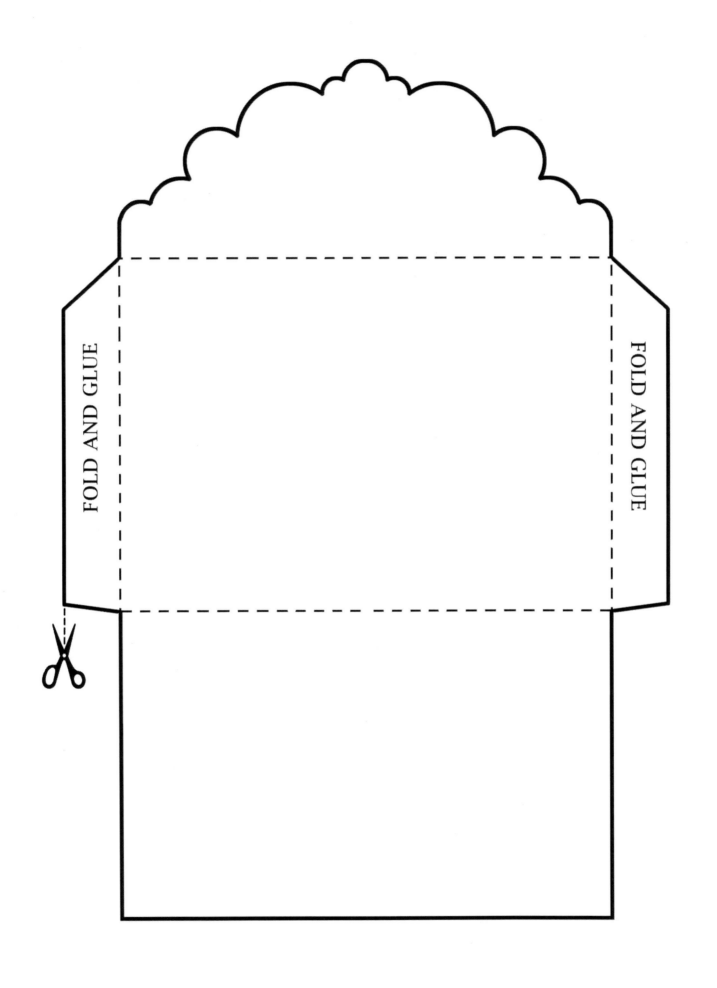

FOLD AND GLUE

FOLD AND GLUE

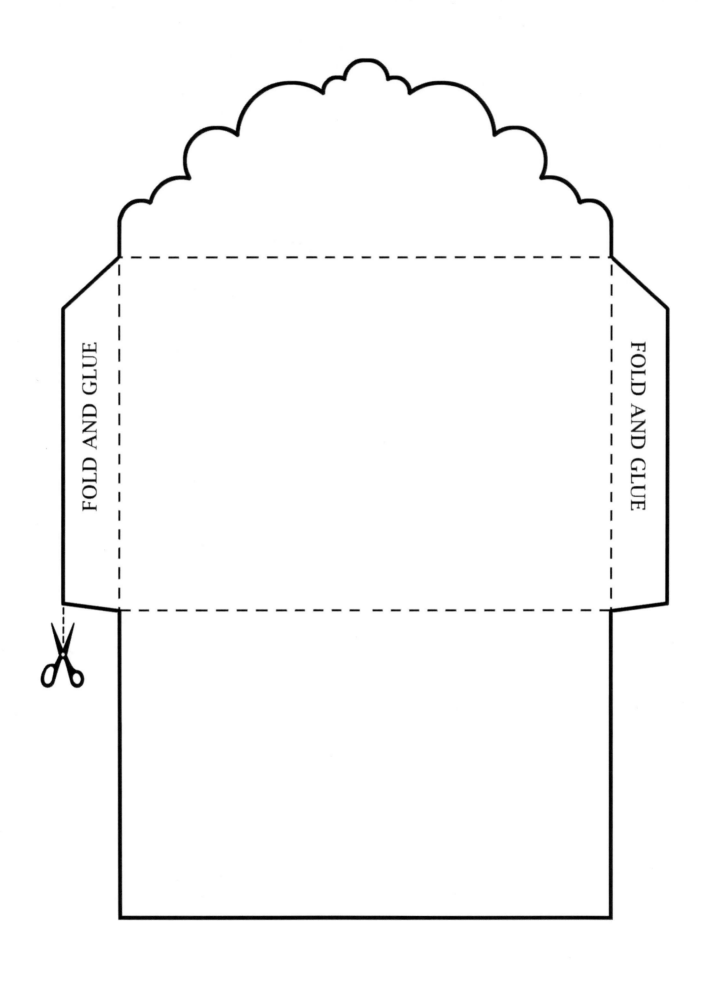

FOLD AND GLUE

FOLD AND GLUE

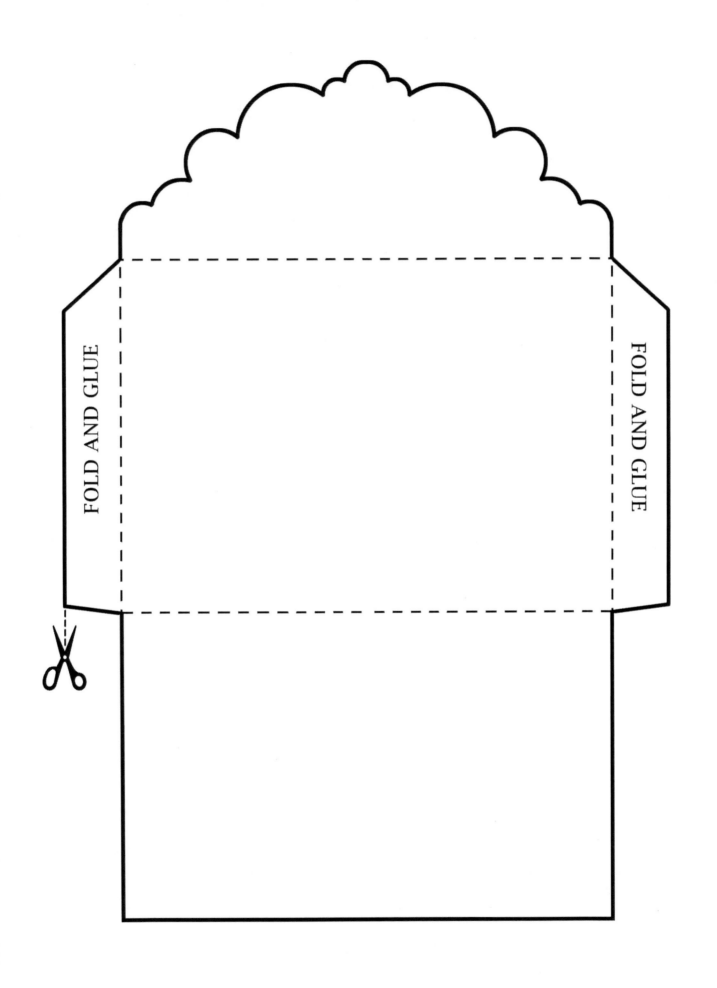

FOLD AND GLUE

FOLD AND GLUE

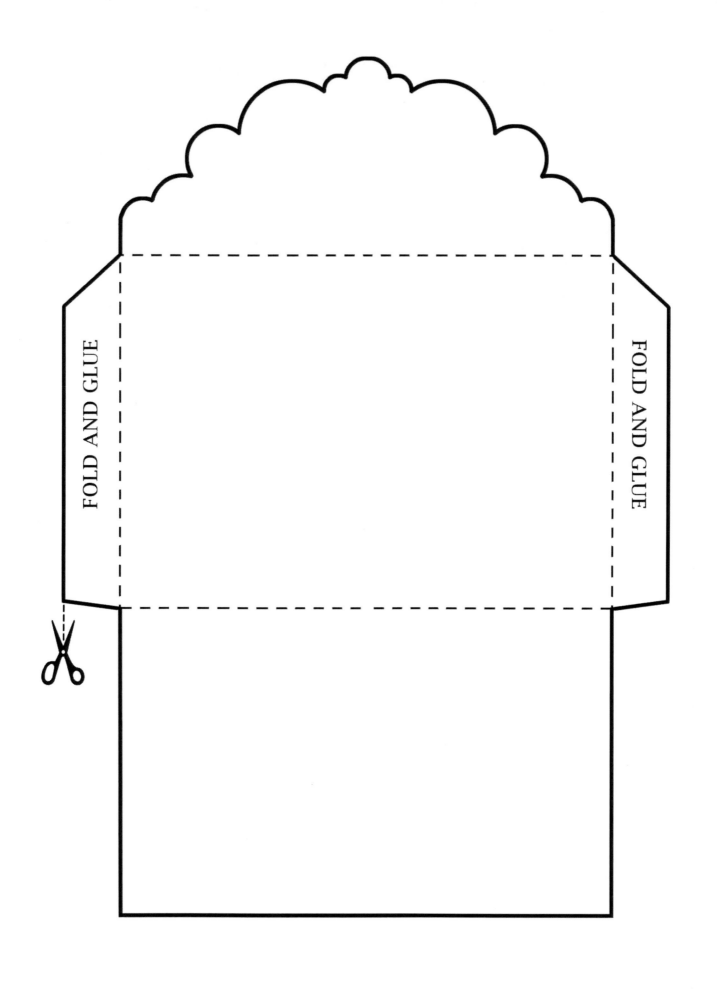

FOLD AND GLUE

FOLD AND GLUE

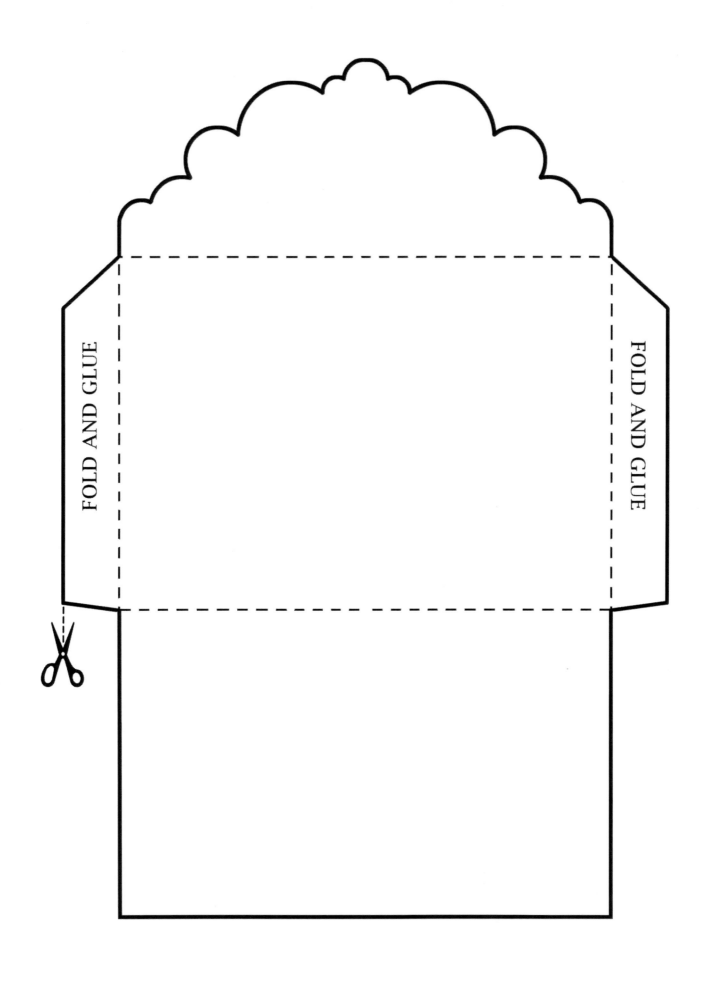

FOLD AND GLUE

FOLD AND GLUE

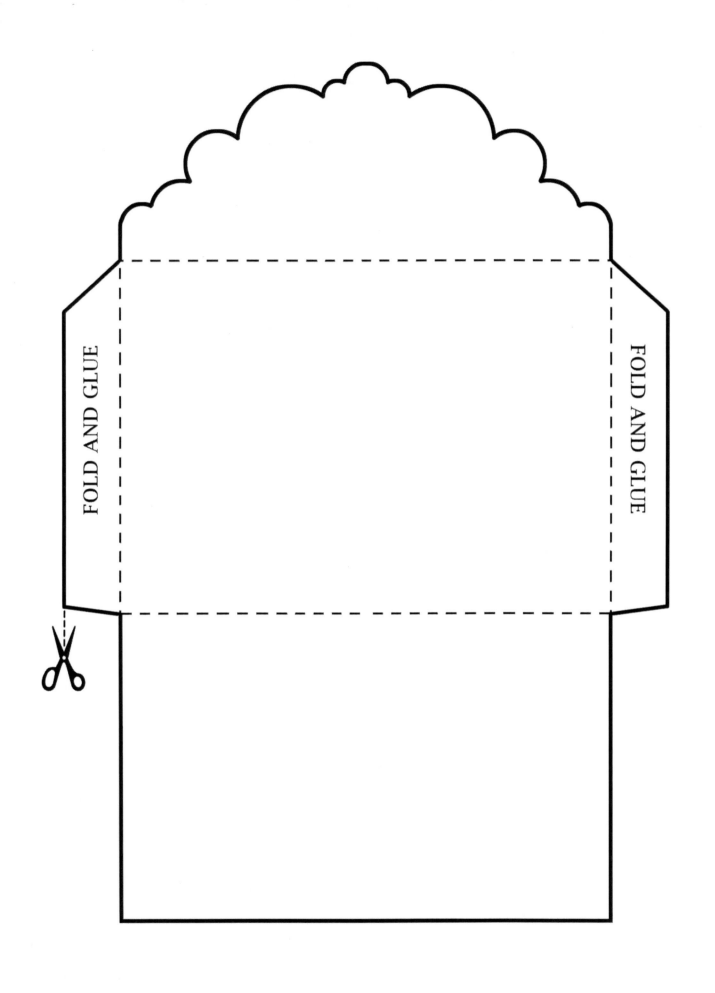

FOLD AND GLUE

FOLD AND GLUE

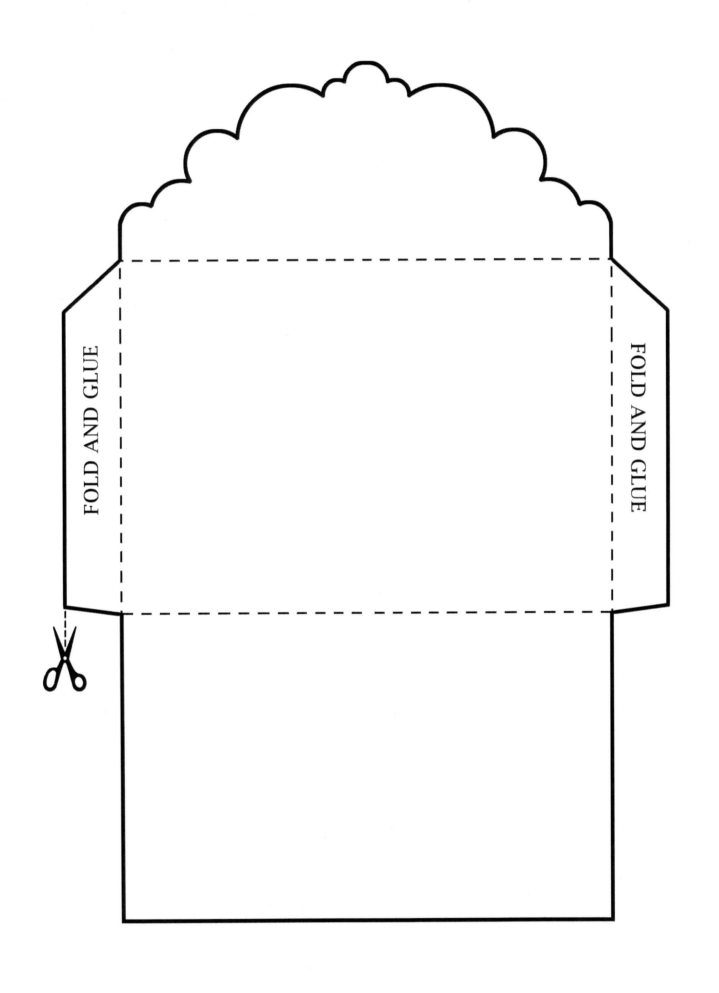

FOLD AND GLUE

FOLD AND GLUE

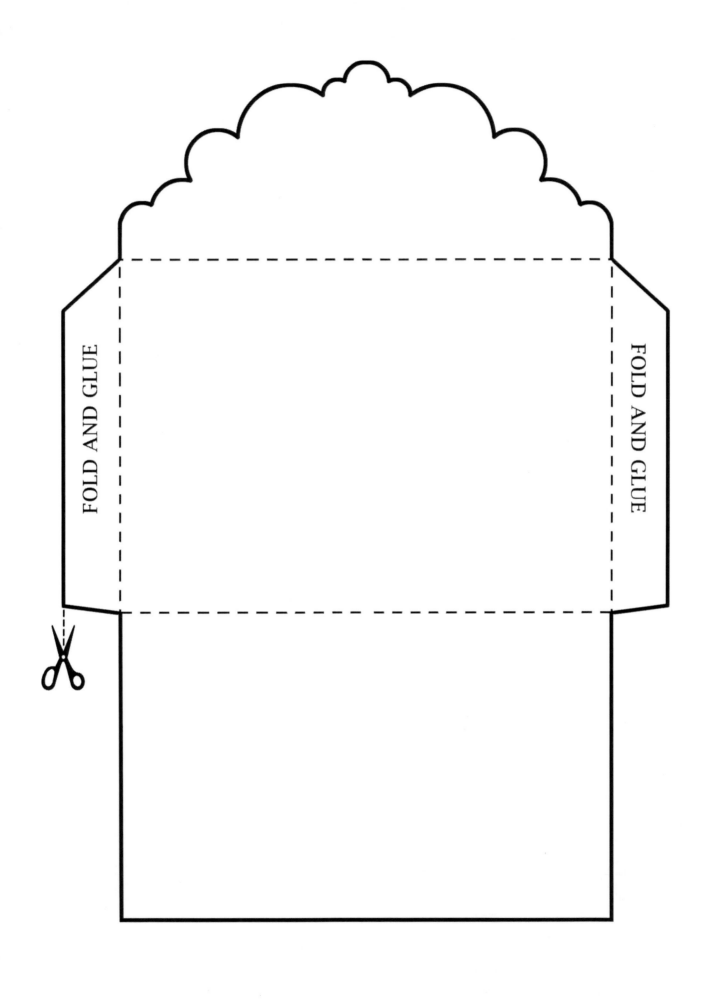

FOLD AND GLUE

FOLD AND GLUE

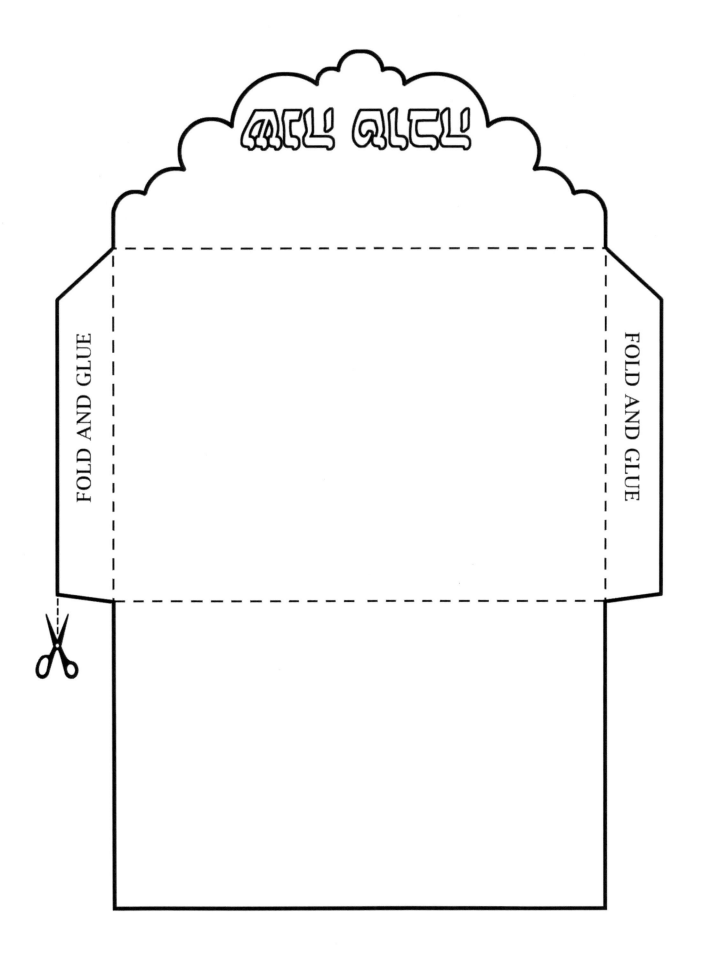

ਆਈਏ ਆਈਏ

FOLD AND GLUE

FOLD AND GLUE

Dear reader,
Thank you so much for purchasing my book,
I hope you enjoyed it.
I will appreciate if you can leave a review on AMAZON.
Hope to see you soon.
HAPPY HOLIDAYS!
Alex

Made in United States
North Haven, CT
11 September 2023

41425463R00087